Fluffy the Vulture seeks to illustrate how similar languages are through the use of color-coded parallel translations.

Fluffy hopes this will encourage you to learn a new language.

Visit FluffyTheVulture.com to listen to the story read aloud in each of the languages, and follow along in the book!

Chinese
English
Spanish
Hindi
Hebrew
Arabic
French
Russian
Japanese

蓬松的秃鹰
Fluffy the Vulture
Fluffy el Buitre
कोमल गिद्ध
פלאפי הנשר
النسر المنفوش
Fluffy le vautour
Пушистый коршун
コンドルのフラッフィー

a collection of words and drawings
by
William Zicker

Call unto me, and I will answer thee, and shew thee great and mighty things, which thou knowest not.

Jeremiah 33:3

Fluffy the Vulture & Count Ten, Fluffy the Vulture 2 in 1

ISBN 978-0-9842655-1-0

Published by Belifan
http://www.belifan.com

© 2009 William Zicker

Thank you to all whose gracious provision of language skills, enthusiasm, encouragement, and smiles helped make this book a reality, including Timmy, Ella, Hannah, Madame Z., Ligia, Wenan, Ashish, Moti, Armando, Gina, Anth, and every one of my family and friends!

Gun robh math agad Robyn

蓬松的秃鹰平息下来睡觉。

Fluffy the Vulture settles down to sleep.

Fluffy el Buitre se acomodo para dormir.

कोमल गिद्ध सोने के लिए आराम से बैठता है।

פלאפי הנשר נשכב לישון

النسر المنفوش يجلس لينام.

Fluffy le vautour s'installe pour dormir.

Пушистый коршун укладывается спать.

コンドルのフラッフィーは、ゆったりすわってねむります。

蓬松的秃鹰在阳光下伸展他的翅膀。

Fluffy the Vulture stretches his wings in the sun.

Fluffy el Buitre extiende sus alas al sol.

कोमल गिद्ध धूप में अपने पंखों को फैलाता है।

פלאפי הנשר מותח את הכנפיים בשמש

النسر المنفوش يفرد جناحيه في الشمس.

Fluffy le vautour étend ses ailes au soleil.

Пушистый коршун расправляет свои крылья на солнце.

コンドルのフラッフィーは、日のひかりにつばさをのばします。

蓬松的秃鹰在风中，盘旋上山。

Fluffy the Vulture rides the wind around the mountains.

Fluffy el Buitre vuela alrededor de las montañas.

कोमल गिद्ध पहाड़ों के चारों ओर हवा के साथ ऊपर उड़ता है।

פלאפי הנשר רוכב על גבי הרוח מסביב להר

النسر المنفوش يجول في الرياح حول الجبال.

Fluffy le vautour monte au vent autour des montagnes.

Пушистый коршун несется с ветром вокруг гор.

コンドルのフラッフィーは、かぜにのって山をまわります。

蓬松的秃鹰感觉气流在他的翅膀边。

Fluffy the Vulture feels the airflow over his wings.

Fluffy el Buitre siente el flujo de aire sobre sus alas.

कोमल गिद्ध अपने पंखों के ऊपर वहती हवा महसूस करता है।

פלאפי הנשר מרגיש את הרוח בכנפיים שלו

النسر المنفوش يشعر بتدفق الهواء على جناحيه.

Fluffy le vautour sent le courant atmosphérique sur ses ailes.

Пушистый коршун чувствует, как его крылья обдувает ветром.

コンドルのフラッフィーは、つばさにかぜのながれをかんじます。

蓬松的秃鹰在田间看到许多颜色。

Fluffy the Vulture sees colors in a field.

Fluffy el Buitre ve colores en un campo.

कोमल गिद्ध मैदान में रंगों को देखता है।

פלאפי הנשר רואה צבעים במגרש

النسر المنفوش يرى ألواناً في حقل.

Fluffy le vautour voit des couleurs dans un champ.

Пушистый коршун видит в поле разные цвета.

コンドルのフラッフィーは、のはらのいろを見ます。

蓬松的秃鹰在他身边闻着花朵。

Fluffy the Vulture smells the flowers around him.

Fluffy el Buitre huele las flores a su alrededor.

कोमल गिद्ध अपने आसपास के फूलों को सूंघता है।

פלאפי הנשר מריח את הפרחים מסביבו

النسر المنفوش يشمّ الأزهار من حوله.

Fluffy le vautour sent les fleurs autour de lui.

Пушистый коршун нюхает цветы вокруг себя.

コンドルのフラッフィーは、まわりの花のにおいをかぎます。

蓬松的秃鹰从一棵树上看着河。

Fluffy the Vulture watches the river from a tree.

Fluffy el Buitre mira el río desde un árbol.

कोमल गिद्ध पेड़ से नदी को ध्यान से देखता है।

פלאפי הנשר רואה את הנהר ממרומי העץ

النسر المنفوش ينظر إلى النهر من أعلى شجرة.

Fluffy le vautour regarde la rivière d'un arbre.

Пушистый коршун любуется рекой с дерева.

コンドルのフラッフィーは、木の上から川をながめます。

蓬松的秃鹰跟随大象一段时间。

Fluffy the Vulture follows an elephant for a while.

Fluffy el Buitre sigue un elefante por un tiempo.

कोमल गिद्ध कुछ समय तक एक हाथी के पीछे उड़ता है।

פלאפי הנשר עוקב אחרי פיל למעט זמן

النسر المنفوش يتبع فيلاً لفترة من الزمن.

Fluffy le vautour suit un éléphant pendant quelque temps.

Пушистый коршун следует какое-то время за слоном.

コンドルのフラッフィーは、しばらくぞうについていきます。

蓬松的秃鹰在长颈鹿上盘旋。

Fluffy the Vulture makes a turn above a giraffe.

Fluffy el Buitre hace un giro por encima de una jirafa.

कोमल गिद्ध एक जिराफ के ऊपर मुड़ता है।

פלאפי הנשר עורך סיור על הג'ירפה ממרומים

النسر المنفوش يدور من فوق زرافة.

Fluffy le vautour fait un tour au-dessus d'une girafe.

Пушистый коршун огибает сверху жирафа.

コンドルのフラッフィーは、キリンの上でぐるっとまわります。

蓬松的秃鹰在风中走向城市。

Fluffy the Vulture rides the wind toward the town.

Fluffy el Buitre vuela hacia la ciudad.

कोमल गिद्ध हवा के साथ शहर की तरफ उड़ता है।

פלאפי הנשר מעופף לכיוון העיר

النسر المنفوش يجول في الرياح نحو المدينة.

Fluffy le vautour monte au vent vers la ville.

Пушистый коршун летит с ветром в сторону города.

コンドルのフラッフィーは、かぜにのって町のほうへいきます。

蓬松的秃鹰在城市吃比萨饼。

Fluffy the Vulture eats a pizza in the town.

Fluffy el Buitre come una pizza en la ciudad.

कोमल गिद्ध शहर में एक पीज़ा खाता है।

פלאפי הנשר אוכל פיצה בעיר

النسر المنفوش يأكل بيتزا في المدينة.

Fluffy le vautour mange une pizza en ville.

Пушистый коршун ест в городе пиццу.

コンドルのフラッフィーは、町でピザをたべます。

蓬松的秃鹰在下午的太阳得到一些休息。

Fluffy the Vulture gets some rest in the afternoon sun.

Fluffy el Buitre descansa en la tarde soleada.

कोमल गिद्ध दोपहर बाद की धूप में थोड़ा आराम करता है।

פלאפי הנשר לוקח תנומה אחר הצהריים

النسر المنفوش يأخذ قسطاً من الراحة تحت شمس بعد الظهر.

Fluffy le vautour se repose dans le soleil de l'après-midi.

Пушистый коршун наслаждается коротким отдыхом в лучах полуденного солнца.

コンドルのフラッフィーは、ごごの日ざしの中でひとやすみします。

蓬松的秃鹰在湖上访问他的朋友。

Fluffy the Vulture visits his friends at the lake.

Fluffy el Buitre visita sus amigos en el lago.

कोमल गिद्ध झील पर अपने दोस्तों से मुलाकात करता है।

פלאפי הנשר מבקר חברים ליד האגם

النسر المنفوش يزور أصدقاءه في البحيرة.

Fluffy le vautour visite ses amis au bord du lac.

Пушистый коршун навещает на озере своих друзей.

コンドルのフラッフィーは、みずうみにいるともだちにあいにいきます。

蓬松的秃鹰与来访的红鹳享受。

Fluffy the Vulture enjoys visiting with the flamingos.

Fluffy el Buitre goza visitando a los flamencos.

कोमल गिद्ध हंसों के साथ मुलाकात का आनन्द लेता है।

פלאפי הנשר נהנה לבקר עם הפלמינגו

النسر المنفوش يستمتع بزيارة طيور البشروش.

Fluffy le vautour jouit les rencontres des flamants.

Пушистый коршун радостно общается с фламинго.

コンドルのフラッフィーは、フラミンゴにあってたのしみます。

蓬松的秃鹰在空中思考他的那一天。

Fluffy the Vulture soars thinking about his day.

Fluffy el Buitre vuela alto pensando en su día.

कोमल गिद्ध अपने दिन के बारे में सोच कर ऊँची उड़ान भरता है।

פלאפי הנשר מרחף וחושב על היום שעבר

النسر المنفوش يحلّق وهو يفكّر بيومه.

Fluffy le vautour s'envole en pensant à son jour.

Пушистый коршун взмывает ввысь, вспоминая события минувшего дня.

コンドルのフラッフィーは、きょうのことをかんがえながら空たかくとびます。

Videos of Fluffy the Vulture being read in each of the nine languages are available at FluffyTheVulture.com and on the Internet Archive, at Archive.org.

fluffythevulture.com

艺术品
artwork
obras de arte
चित्रकला
אמנות
الأعمال الفنية
des oeuvres d'art
Произведения искусства
いろえ

蓬松的秃鹰
Fluffy the Vulture
Fluffy el Buitre
कोमल गिद्ध
פלאפי הנשר
النسر المنفوش
Fluffy le vautour
Пушистый коршун
コンドルのフラッフィー

大象
elephant
elefante
हाथी के
פיל
الفيل
éléphant
за слоном
ぞう

长颈鹿
giraffe
jirafa
जिराफ
הג'ירפה
الزرافة
girafe
жирафа
キリン

长颈鹿
giraffe
jirafa
जिराफ़
גַ'ירָפָה
زرافة
girafe
жираф
キリン

This book, "Count Ten, Fluffy the Vulture" is the second in a series of books for children.

Videos of the first book, "Fluffy the Vulture," being read in each of nine languages are available at FluffyTheVulture.com and on the Internet Archive, at Archive.org.

fluffythevulture.com

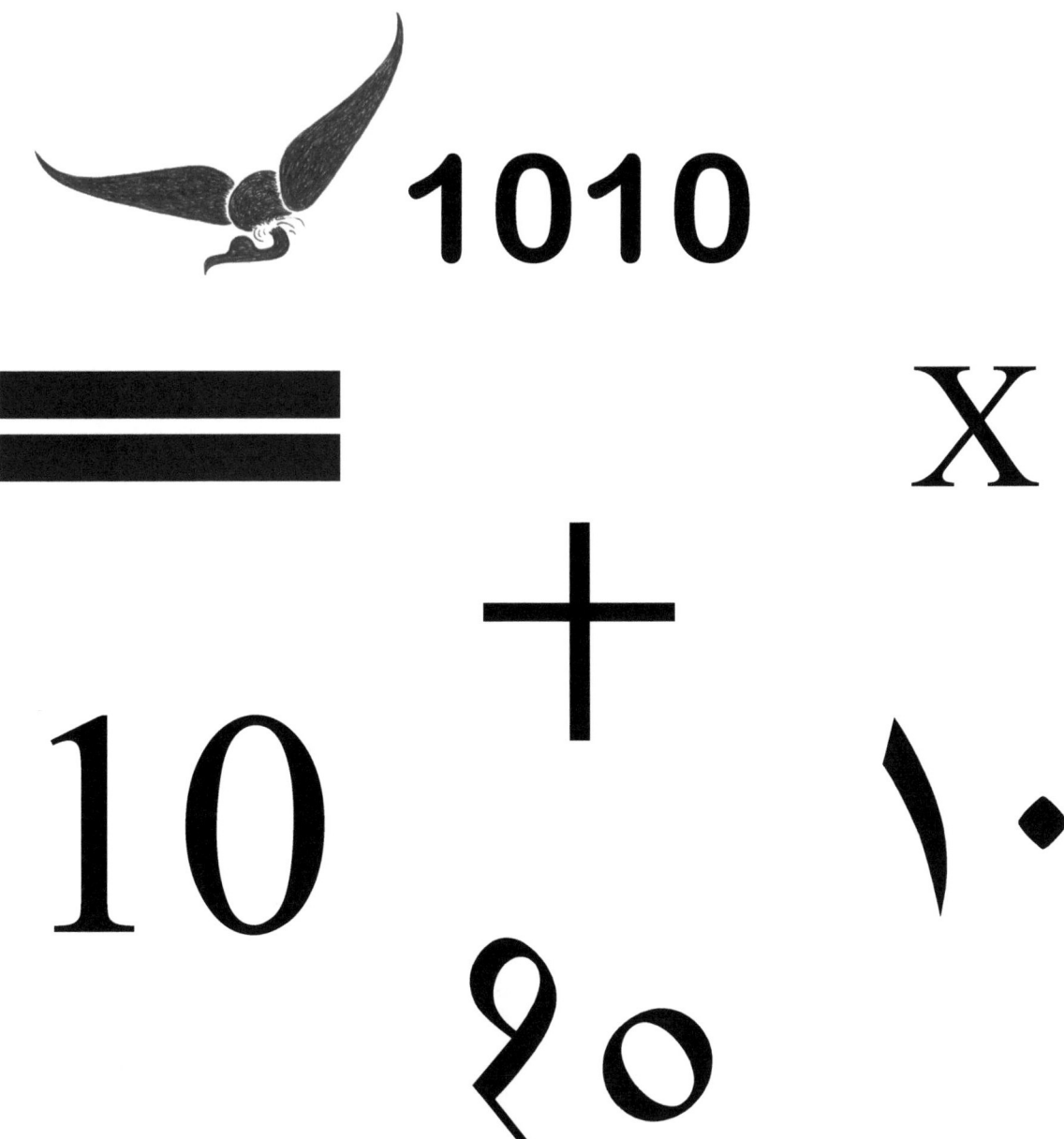

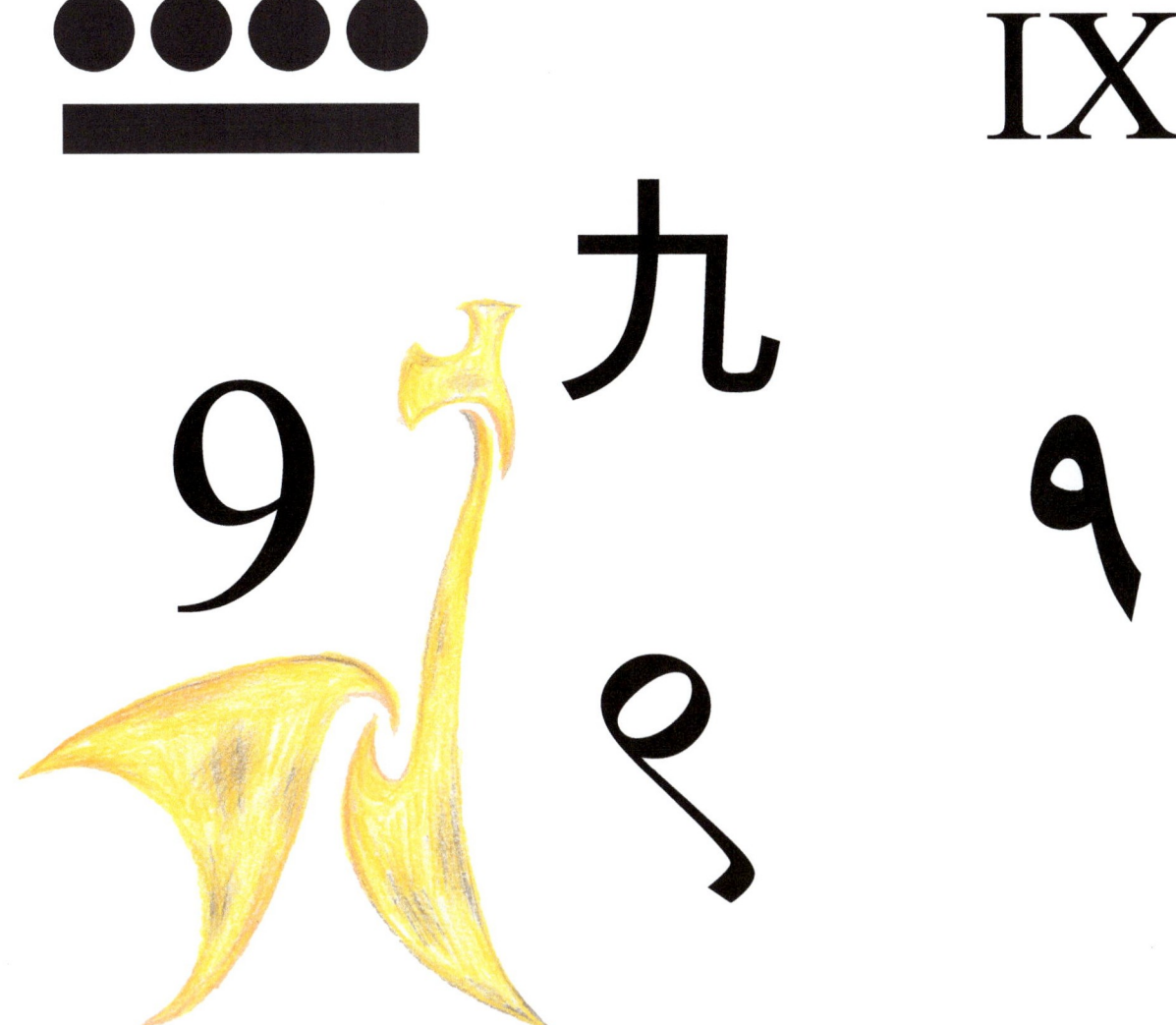

111

𒐌

VII

七

7

٧

௯

110

÷ VI
六
6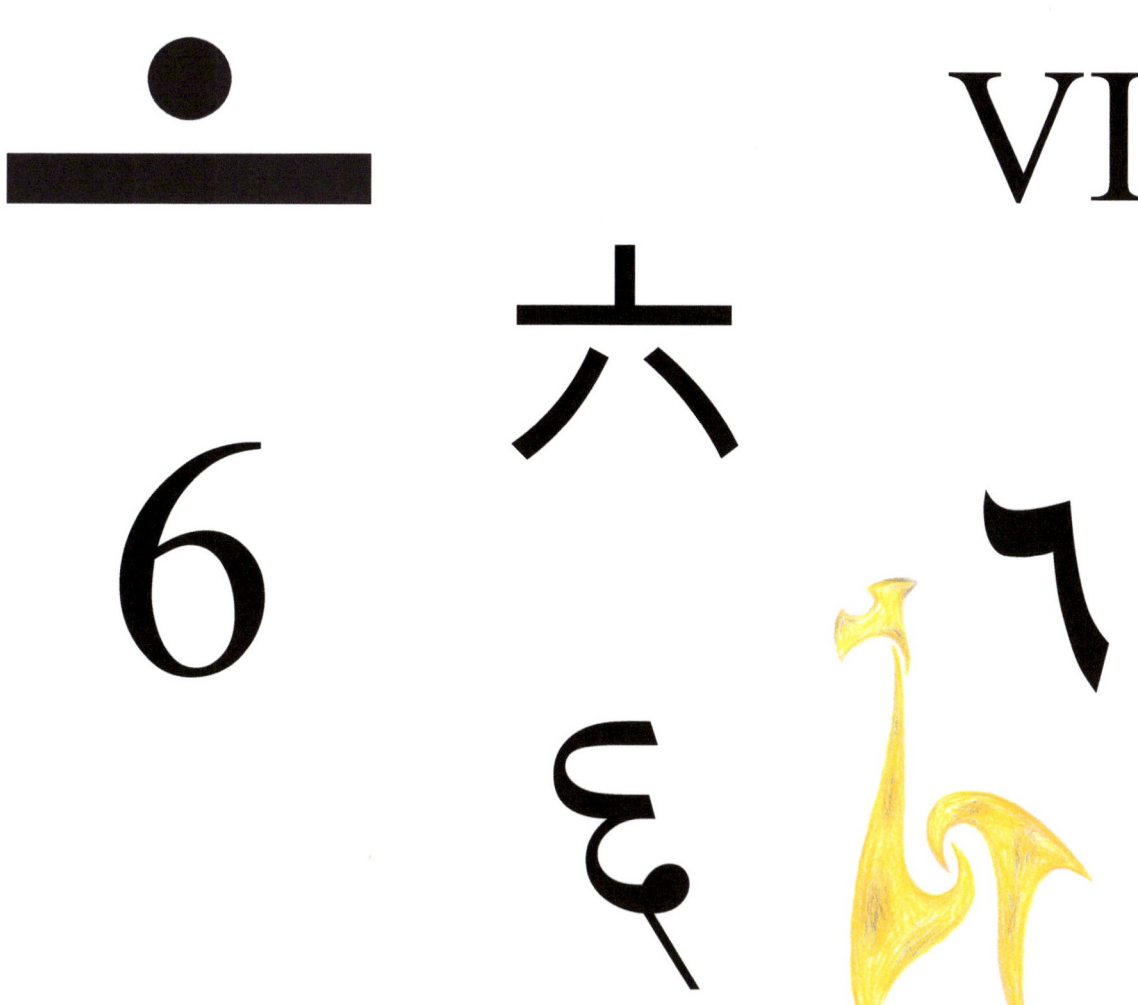

101

五　V

5　૦

૫

100

●●●●

IV

四

4

٤

𐎗

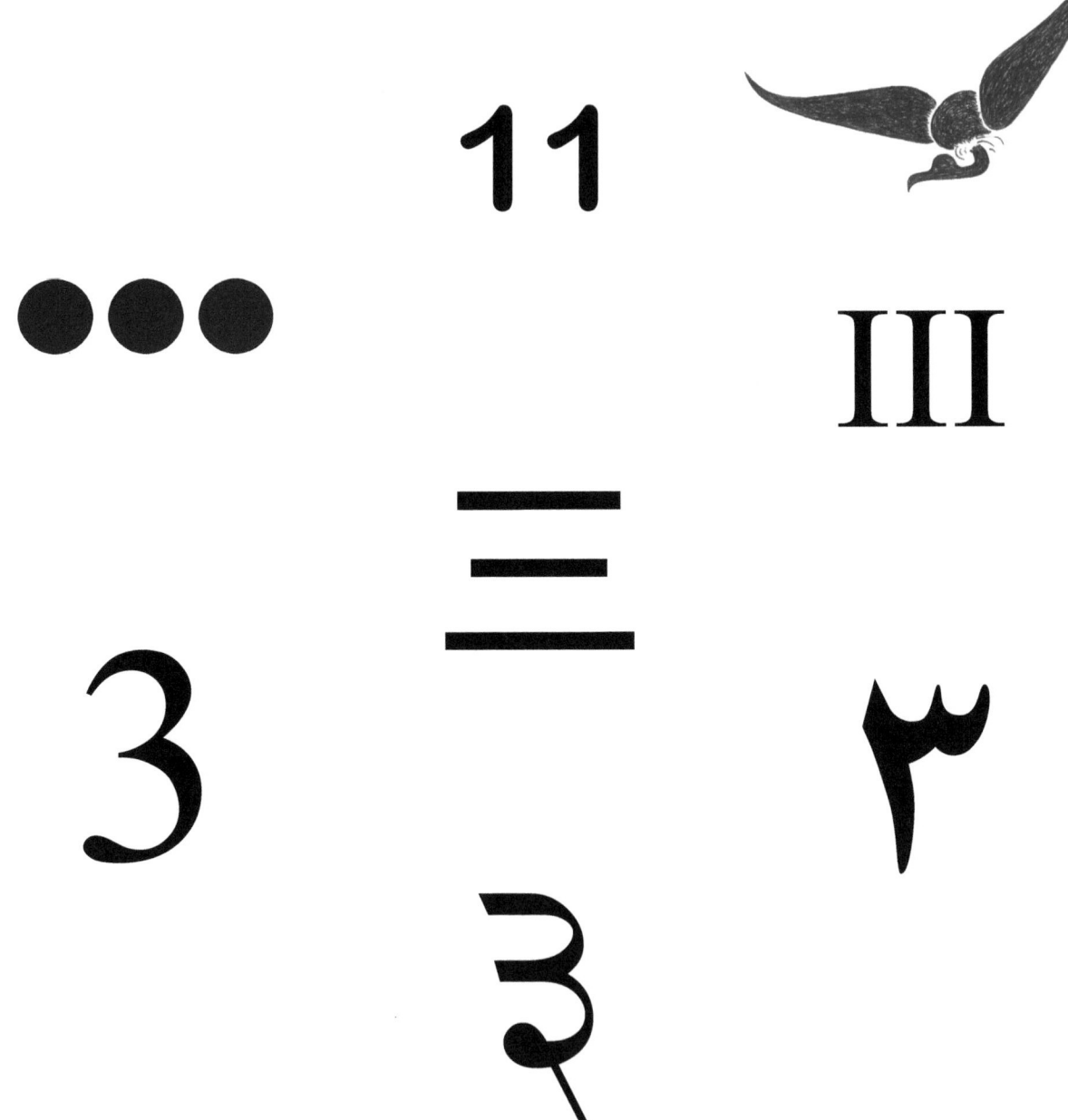

$$\frac{10}{2} = \frac{\text{II}}{٢}$$

$$\frac{1}{1}$$

$$\bullet \frac{1}{1} \frac{1}{8})$$

$$\frac{\ddot{}}{2} = \frac{10}{\mathrm{چ}} = \frac{\mathrm{II}}{٣}$$

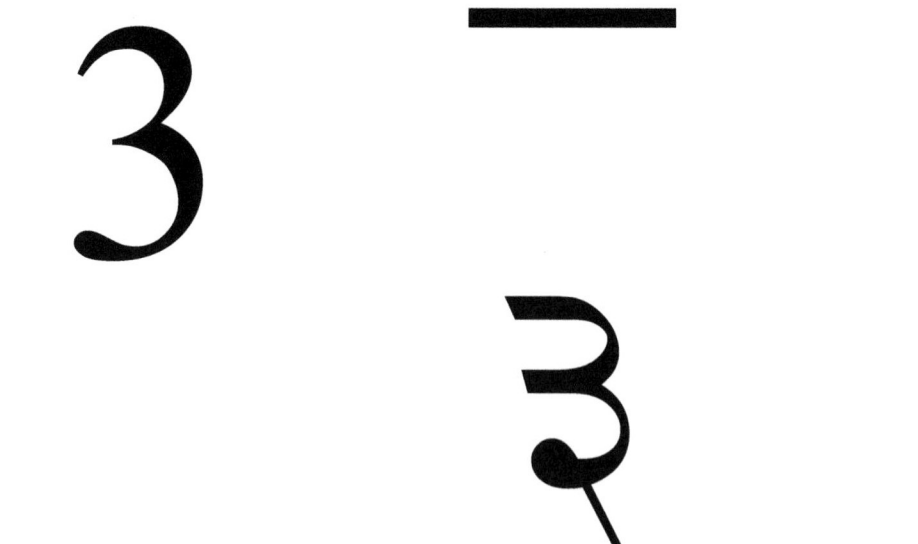

100

●●●● IV

四

4 ٤

𐎡

101

五 V

5 ٥

۴

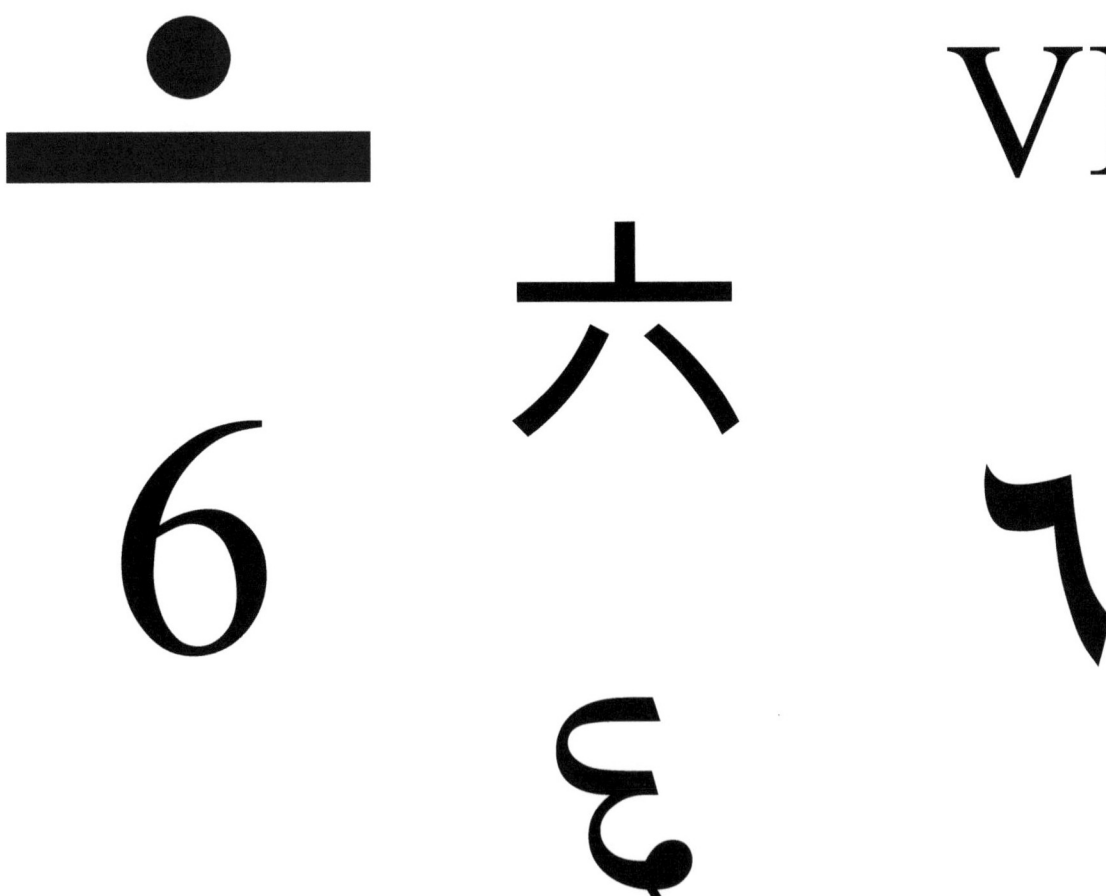

111

⠒

VII

७

7

૭

1001

九

IX

9

٩

۹

$$1010 = 10 + 10 \times \wedge\cdot$$

binary
1010

mayan
≡

roman
X

chinese
✝

10
european

١٠
arabic

१०
hindi

Seven different number systems are used to count the leaves.

Look for similarities among the numbers!

All of these systems have a number zero except Roman.

There are other number systems more limited in use, or no longer used.

Can you count the leaves along with Fluffy the Vulture?

Thank you to all whose encouragement and ideas helped bring Fluffy the Vulture back in a second book, including my co-author, and as before every one of my family and friends!

Gun robh math agad Robyn

But they that wait upon the LORD shall renew their strength; they shall mount up with wings as *vultures*; they shall run, and not be weary; and they shall walk, and not faint.

Isaiah 40:31

(originally in Hebrew, this passage from the Bible contains a word that is commonly translated "eagles," the same word as that for "vultures")

```
                    Published by Belifan
                    http://www.belifan.com

                    © 2009 William Zicker
```

count ten

Chinese	蓬松的秃鹰
English	Fluffy the Vulture
Spanish	Fluffy el Buitre
Hindi	कोमल गिद्ध
Hebrew	פלאפי הנשר
Arabic	النسر المنفوش
French	Fluffy le vautour
Russian	Пушистый коршун
Japanese	コンドルのフラッフィー

a collection of numbers and drawings
by
William & Robyn Zicker

Fluffy the Vulture sees a giraffe eating leaves from a tree, then watches as the leaves grow back!

Can you count the leaves with Fluffy?

Visit FluffyTheVulture.com for more fun!